I0624650

Life Poetry

By

Kuhlula Ngobeni

Life Poetry

Published by
Blessed Thabang Mobosi
Nkomaneni Dan C House No 0601
Postal Address: PO Box 3275
Tzaneen 0850 Limpopo
South Africa

Email: Blessed.btm@gmail.com
Telephone 072 875 6983
Cell: 061 953 9726 / 067 817 2911

1ST Edition

ISBN: 978-0-6399345-9-4

Life Poetry

About the Writer

Kuhlula Ngobeni was born on 08 June 1998. His hobby is football. His passion is helping people to see how special they are and how optimism can lead to greatness as well on how it helps them in moving forward with their lives. He believes his calling is to become a social worker in which he wishes to pursue as a career. He admires Pastor Dennis Ngobeni and T.D Jakes as his role models.

Table of Contents

About the Writer 5

Pain 9

Love 10

God 11

Life 12

Poverty..13

Music 15

JOY 16

TIME..18

LOVE..20

WATER 21

Race 22

Money..24

PARENTS 25

EDUCATION..26

WISDOM 27

PRISON..28

THE QUESTION OF LOVE 29

MY DREAM GIRL 30

PUSH 31

THE ANGEL I MATE 32

The Journey of Breathing...33

RESPECT AND NOBLENESS...34

LOVE..35

  The Pain of Being Dumped 36

  To Accept 37

  DREAMING BIG 38

  Anger 39

  INTROSPECTION..40

  People Are Not the Same..41

  Tears 42

  You Are Always a Person 43

  Questioning..44

  Death 46

  Take action...47

  A Dog 48

  Smile 49

  BROKEN PROMISE..50

Eyes Acts 52

FIRST TIME FASCINATION 53

MY CRUSH...54

MY DREAM GIRL 55

THE BLIND PERSON 56

A Recall to the Past 57

Pain

Where do you come from?
Who sent you to us?
Who are you pain?
From all the corners of the earth
People cry because of you.
People suffer in your presents.
Hatred is the produce of your presents
Tears overflow because of your presents,
Cries and groans are heard because of your
presents.

From animals you are there,
From human beings you are there
From young people you are there
From old people you are there
Ooh pain, where do you belong?

We drink medication to stop you
We go to churches to stop you
We go to In'angas to stop you
Pain in all our ways you reject to be stopped
But you choose to deteriorate,
we are tired of you.

Love

What are you love?
What kind of feelings are you?
Why are you so uncontrollable?
You are love and you sound good

You are praised,
You are being sang day and night
You are invited in many lives
You can't be seen or touched but you can be felt
You are a good feeling.

You bring people together
You are unity
You make haters to love
You bring smiles between people
You produce offspring.
You are so astonishing.

Your presents means joy
Your presents means unity
Your presents means marriage,
Your presents means peace
Ooh love, ooh love you truly come from God
And truly you are God in action.

God

You are the creator of the uncreated
The unchangeable changer
Eternal and infinity
You are god, yes you are my god.
The alpha and the omega,
The alpha of the alphas,
You are God

You are a mother to the motherless
You are a father to the fatherless
You are a friend to the friendless

You are God in good and in bad times.
The earth is your footstool,
The earth is the work of your hands
The believers find their heart desires in you.
Ooh lord of lords,
Ooh king of kings,

You are God of everything.
You are a spirit
You are love and kindness,
You are the way where there is no way,
You are the light in the darkness,
You're the past, presents and the future.
The birds sing, the frogs sings, people sing,
All creations sing,
All creations are the work of your hands.
You are God indeed you are god.

Life

Life is push and pull
Life you are not fair, but you are good,
You are so confusing, but we choose you than
death.
From day to day we wait to push and to pull you.
From the belly of the earth to the corners of the
earth you are
Moving day and night
Life you are not fair, but we get used to it

You are not enjoyable sometimes
You are full of pain, sorrow, cries and groans.
You don't speak but you make people to talk about
you.
You are simple breathing.
Everyone needs you
Everyone fears you

Why can't we all be wealthy?
Why can't we have our loved once?
Your directions are undefined
Your anger is death
Your joy is birth.
Impilo emhlabeni.
We pray but you are still tough
You acknowledgement brings stress in some cases.
When you are angry you cause cries and groans.

Poverty

Poverty you're the opposite of wealth.
Are you a living thing?
Do you talk with people?
Where do you come from?
You are called poverty.

Why can't we all be rich?
Why can't we all have massive houses?
Why can't we all have houses?
We say no to you poverty.

Your presence is hunger
Your presence is thirstiness
Your presence is tears, cries and groans.
Your presence is not welcomed.
We never invited you on earth but you are dancing
in our lives.
From the belly of the earth you are produced only to
bring lack of joy to people.

You are a pain cause
You're the cause sickness
You are destruction
You are a thief of joy to some.

You steal peoples hope
You close people's eyes
You limit people's ability
You remove dignity and create a bugger

You are poverty
You are negative
We say no
We can't make you feel comfortable in our lives.

Music

Your presents is dance
A beat of joy
A beat of peace
A beat of togetherness

A melody that heals wounds
That changes feelings
You are so touching.

Life saviour,
A best doctor you're.
You can touch but you can't be touched.
You can move people from one emotion to another emotion,

From one movement to another movement.
You are simply the tempo, the beat and the tune.
A simple melody,
A simple sound,
Melody filled up of power to amend lives.

JOY

Everyone wants you
Everyone fight for you
Everyone fights to have you
You can't be seen moving
But you can only be felt.
Can't be touched,
Youre the feeling of happiness

In your presence there is joy peace and happiness
You are so sweet when you flow.
What a joyous feeling you are.

Fears may be there,
Cries and groans may be there
Struggles and sufferings may be there
Sadness may be there
But joy cometh in the morning

You are simple but many lack you.
Humans, animals and plants all want you.
All creatures seek you.
When you come you don't knock, but you change
lives and lives, pain and cries
Loneliness and sadness
Joy you are simple but hard to be found.

Are you a living thing?
Do you speak?

You are the feelings in emotions,
You are simple but hard to be found.
Joy cometh in the morning.

TIME

who are you?
What are you?
Where are you going?
Why are you so unfair?
you are the past, the present and the future.
Why don't you wait for us?
Why do you move so fast?

Day and night you move
Any second we miss is a lose,
Any minute we miss is a waste,
Any hour we miss is regret,
Any day that we miss is a lose,
Any week we miss is a stress,
Any month we miss sadness,
Any year we miss is unforgettable.

You are a second that can't be replaced,
You are a minutes that can't be replaced,
You the hours that can't be replaced,
You are a day that can't be replaced,
You are weeks that can't be replaced,
You are a months that can't be replaced,
 You are a years that can't be replaced,

Time never gets tired of moving,
Time waits for nobody,

Time is money,
Time is loss or gain
You do not change, but everything changes you go
Time is the holder of life
You are time, tick, tick, tick, tick, you are time.

Nobody can bribe you. For you don't communicate.
Nobody can retreat you, for you are uncontrollable.
Nobody can balance you
For you are for yourself
Time wasted never regain
You are time, the past, present and the future.

LOVE

Love is a feeling,
Love is blind
Love is sweet, but sometimes is sower
Love is a passion and a sense.

It's hard to love someone and not be loved in return.
But the most painful thing is to love someone and
never get the chance and courage to tell that person
how much you feel.
Love can't get tired so easily,
Love can't be stopped; it is not by dearth only,
Love is sweet, but sometimes its sower.

For many times we shout love,
For many times we cry for love,
For many times we kill for love,
For many times we hate for love,
For many times we are deceived for love,
Love is sweet but sometimes is sower.

Never get tired if you still want to try,
For you never know the time you will get yes.
Love is an assent on a sense.
Love is a passion moving from the heart.
Love is a feeling.
Described in many ways, but you have one true
definition which is feelings.
Which is to protect and to care, passion adoring.
Love is sweet, but sometimes is sower.

WATER

Water is liquid and soft.
It moves from the hand to the mouth
From the hand to the stomach
From the stomach to the face
Face is flowing with tears
Tears caused by an incident and pain
Water you're an important liquid.

You are the mother of saint on people's life
You are the mother of life
The stream flows with life because of you!
The tears flow
The blood flows.
The acids move out of our bodies
The plants grow

You are natural, colourless, and Shapeless
You are the power of mixture and chemistry.
Your name is water

Race

A race is a competition,
A race needs speed,
 A race need time management
A race is competition in a journey.

Those who are in a race always get tired.
Tiredness is a way signifying working hard.
Working in a race that need a choice
Traveling is made by one choice
One choice gives one step
One step gives another step
The race

Thousands steps start with one step.
When you take a step never retreat.
A step can be determined by anything
As long as you are going forward that is a race.

Keep on running
Keep on moving forward.
Forward in a race is always forward.
If you are tired of running then walk
If you are tired of walking, then crawl.
If you are tired of crawling, then roll down

Sometimes some people may always be forward to
you, you must not give up your race.
Being left behind in a race does not mean you will
always be left behind,

Work up your acceleration
Work up your tiredness
Work up your dream.

Give your life to finish your race.
Keep on moving, push is the ability.

Money

Money is the root of evil
Money the success of our lives
Money the destructor,
Money the advocator,
Money the life destroyer,
You are silver and gold.

We say money is the root of evil, but we all want to
get jobs to find money.
Day and night we compete for money,
Day and night we kill for money,
Day and night we are deceived for money,
Day and night we become evil because of money.

Money what are you.
Why can't we all have you?
What makes you so noble?
Where are you going to end up?

You don't talk, but we talk about you
You don't change, but you change people's life.
The easy way you come is the easy way you go
The hard way you come is the hard way you go.
Money who are you?

PARENTS

What a wonderful gift you are
You are a valuable object
Very much protective.
Having you is a gift
Lacking you is never a gif, t but the opportunity to
increase ones effort.

You provide while you are hustling.
You are children to your parents, but you are
parents to us.
From your sweat we quench our hunger.
It is your money that we spend.

You took struggles for your children
Stress for your children
You faced the trouble we made
You become my strength when am weak
To face my challenges

You are a gift that nobody can doubt
You are a gift that is above all gifts
You are the happiness of your children.

EDUCATION

Education you are the impartation of knowledge
You are the skills and the movement of wisdom.
You are the key to success
You are the mother of luxury
You are the application and curriculum vitae
Education where did you generate?

The future of people is in your hands.
The ability of people is in your ways
Your ways are the ways of prosperity

Doctors and teachers are your children
Police and soldiers are your results
Engineers and lawyers are your fruits
Managers and pilots are your product
Mechanics and scientist are your outcomes
Geologist and sexologist are your works

You make things to happen easy
You improve people's life
You make money in the lives of those who have you.
You don't talk, but we talk about you
We want you. You are education,
Those who lack you invite poverty,
Those who lack you lack skills, wisdom, knowledge
and art.
You are education.

WISDOM

Wisdom you can't be questioned
Questioning you is like rejecting wealthy
Your presence leads to luxurious life

Wisdom carries development
Wisdom carries knowledge
Knowledge carries solutions
Knowledge is the motor of wisdom

Those who seek wisdom find prosperity
Those who seek wisdom find wealthy
We need wisdom to solve our problems
We need wisdom to go to our better future
Wisdom who are you for many reject you not
knowing that you are the future.
Many hate you not knowing that you are everything
they need.

You are the eyes of the moral
You are the skills and abilities.
Those who have you they have rest
Those who have you; they see things differently
We need wisdom, for it hold the better tomorrow

PRISON

Jail is your name.
You are a cage of people's life.
You are full of darkness and pain
You are full of hell and sufferings.
Death can be your fruits.
Pains and groans a your children
Suffering and demolishing is your product,
Tears and tears walk on your path.

You are never good to humans
You are never caring for people
You never gave peace to people
You never bought peace to the world
But yet you are
Produced to bring peace to the world
Old and young perish in you
White and blacks perish in you
Cripples and able perish in you
Blind and death perish in you.

You don't reject any life
But anyone that comes to you
You accept and change the life.

THE QUESTION OF LOVE

What can I say? I am speechless!
What have I done to deserve this pain?
What wrongs did I do to you?
I can do anything only to get you back in my life
Tell me what you want me to do.
Why is love so unfair to me?
You fell in love with me so mightily
You promised not to stop loving me
You took my heart away from me
You told me there's nothing that can separate us
You are the one I love please come back to me.

Our love was an ultimate
Our connection was as of the same blood bond.
Our plays were as spending time in paradise.
Our kisses were so moving
Our souls in peace and joy
Our love………

I can't stop loving you
I can't stop thinking of you
I can't breathe without you
I feel uncompleted without you
My love, please come back to me
No matter how long it takes I will wait for you.
My pillow is always filled up with tears
My mind is troubled because of thinking of you.
My heart beat for you, please come back to me.

MY DREAM GIRL

Your name sounds like an amending music.
You talk as the voice of God is moving in my ears
Meeting you was wondrous blessing
You're an angel sent in my life.
Your acknowledgement brings about peace
Your present is rest
Your acknowledgement is harmony
Your present is joy and giggles.
Your smiles are the best medicine I need.

Before you were in my life I was lost
Myself I never knew.
But all changed in your arrival.
In your smile the beauty of life was revealed
In your touches I felt alive.

Truly you are my soul mate
You're the bone of my bone
The flesh of my flesh
The rib of my rib
You are the joy of my soul.
My thanks to God!
My dream has become a reality

PUSH

Push is a force.
Push can be a solution to many things
Push is mandatory in some activities
Push can be life or death.
Keep on pushing harder.
Just as a woman giving birth to a child
 Push is a must.

Just as living life, for life is push and pull.
Just as going to school push is a must
Keep on pushing harder.

It has many meanings, but to God creatures:
P-pray
U-until
S-something
H-happen

In good and in bad times never stop pushing.
With strength or no strength never stop pushing.
Rejected and being mocked never stop pushing.
Divorced or lost your loved one, keep on pushing.
Life is life, in life you have to push and pull.
Keep on pushing.

If you fail to push you are failing your prosperity and
dream.

THE ANGEL I MATE

Hey girl where do you stay?
You dressed like the government has dressed you.
You look like you are top on the city girls
This beauty looks like walking in the present of God.

Some angels appear unexpectedly!
You are the queen of my heart.
You caught my heart like an unexpected rain

The minute I saw you I felt my life being restored
You are the queen of my heart.
I don't want to depart from you.
Since you are here I feel healthy, spiritually and
physical.

In your presents my blood flows smoothly
In your presents I feel so protected
It's a blessing to be with you
It's a wonderful time to be in your arms
To be with you is like being in heaven
You are the queen of my heart.
I relish and cherish you
I adore and love you.

You are the air that I breathe,
You are the queen of my heart.

The Journey of Breathing

The air that you breathe makes you alive.
Being alive makes you to be in a journey
Being in a journey is a choice, but a not must of life.

Everyone wants to live and that makes us to travel
on the way of life.
Along the journey we flow and climb hills
In all the ways you are in a journey.
We all want to improvements in life which makes
competition.

Competing is part of traveling in life.
Competing is part of the journey
We all know that along the race some give up
Just like a racer who loses strength

Never commit suicide, stay strong as those who are
in a race. Even if you get tired never quit keep on
breathing till you Flow on that hill.
Always know that a journey is filled up by many hills
and But your time to flow will come soon.

RESPECT AND NOBLENESS

Respect and nobleness is not what you choose to have, but is what is given to you when you deserve it.

Don't fight to have what you can't have
Don't choose what is not in a multiple choice
Don't give medals to yourself

Many want to be respected and nobbled
Many want to be worshiped
Many have set themselves to be on top of others
But they all don't know to pay the price needed to be respected and noble.

Never kill to get respect and to be noble
Never be a deceiver to get respect and nobility
Never use bad moral to get respect and nobleness

Why do we kill to be respected?
Is fame better than life?
Why do you want to be respected and noble?
Why are you in the crave to be respected and to a noble?
What will people gain by making you noble?
Respect and being noble is not a choice, but what you get when you deserve it.
We say no to Corruption.

LOVE

A simple feeling and a sense
You can't be changed, but you change people's lives.
Nobody knows your strength, but you are powerful.
You are love, you are hard to get, but you are
everywhere

The Pain of Being Dumped

It's not easy to accept a divorce, but don't kill yourself. It's not easy to be separated from the one you gave your heart to

It's not easy to accept that is the end of the relationship

It's not easy to accept to be left alone, but be strong
Love break up is part of life
Love break up will never be stopped on earth
Love break up is not a choice, but it's a life rotation
Love break up is never good to people
Stay strong in life

What leaves you was never yours
What is yours will never live you
What God joins while is an item will never be separated.
What we can do is to accept that some things can't be recreated.
 Sometimes we lose in order to gain.

To Accept

To accept is to admit and to understand
To accept is a hard decision to make
To accept is to amend your life
To accept is change by moving from the past and heading to the future.
Learn to accept.

As people we tend to do lot of mistakes because of failing to accept.
People kill themselves
People fall into temptations
People are deceived
Accept you will see the future.
Learnt to accept

Sometimes you must know that you can't have power to change some things.
Sometimes you will lose what you love most
Nobody chooses to face hard things
Everyone faces their own lions
Everyone lives own life
Everyone has own capability, potentially and limitations
Know yourself.
Some problems you can't pass them until you accept.

DREAMING BIG

Dreaming is having a goal,
Dreaming is having a purpose to achieve in future
Dreaming big is proposing something big
Dreaming is a step you have to take, for nobody will
dream for you.
Keep on dreaming.

Sometimes the only way to be more prosperous is
by dreaming big.
Sometimes you have to crave for what is far and
behind you.
Sometimes you have to believe in the platform.
Sometimes you have to believe on what is behind
your reality.

The more you dream big is the more you improve
big, Things happen through the process of
dreaming.

Dreaming is the light of the future,
The future will always be doomed if there's no a
dream. A dream without a vision is doomed.
The only way you can reach your goal is by having a
dream.

Anger

You are natural, but dangerous to creatures
You can control but It's not easy to control you
You are nothing but anger
You are full of impolite.

Nobody can tell where it come from
Nobody can change your force
Nobody can stop you from existence

The devil always uses you as his weapon.
Death Is connected with you
Mistakes are connected with you
Regrets are connected with you

Many calls you a devil because you are merciless
Many people change because of you
You are an invisible and untouchable force

Those who control you find favour and peace.
Those who control you benefit in return.
Those who control you avoid troubles.
Those who control you avoid the devil.
Those who control you avoid many dangers.

INTROSPECTION

Introspection is self- examination.
What you see is what you get
What you desire is what you receive,
What you think is who you are.

Being in the middle of people does not make you be like them.
Being in a poor family does not make you poor.
Being judged by your mistakes does not make you a mistake.

Never be discouraged by what you see, but believe in what you fancy.
For the power of the mind is a change of everything.
Never be led by mob psychology,
For you have your own capability and limitations.

The past is not who you are,
The mistakes and the misfortune is not who you are,
Failing does not make you to be a failure,
For failing is part of life showing that you are doing something.

how confusing self- confidence is, the level, and the time to accept.
Never say you can't if you didn't try,
Never say you can't while others can do
Believing is the beginning of every happenstance

People Are Not the Same

People are the creatures of God and the images of God. Sometimes you can conclude that you are born to suffer.

When you see others being wealthy at your age, Your time will come. Sometimes among your friends you can find yourself failing alone, your time will come.

Sometimes people at your age can run faster than you, your time will come. People you are a person in individual.

Everyone has his/her own limits and potential,
Everyone has his/her own problems and solutions,
Everyone has his/her own goals and plans,
Everyone has own gifts and capabilities,
Everyone has his/her own reactions and emotions,
People you are a person in individuals.

Don't compete, but fight to achieve in your life
Win and lose is part of competing.
Never be motivated by the desire to beat other,
rather by the desire to achieve.

Tears

Tears you are simple water.
You flow smoothly while pains eat badly.
You rain simply while, hurts suffer harder.
You are just a water fall twin.

There are tears of pain and tears of joy
But they are called tears.
There's a cry of pain and a cry of joy
But they all produce tears.

Sometimes the solution we need is to release tears
all over the face. Sometimes to reduce our burdens
tears have to come out, Sometimes the only
language we can talk is showing tears.

For many times when our tears fall so is our
problems and agony washed away
When we cry after crying we always feel a change
on what made us to cry.
Crying it can be a problem and it can be a solution.
Let your tears flow if you fill feel so.

You Are Always a Person

Sophisticated or complicated you are still a human.
Stressing or struggling you are still a human.
Cripple or crazy you are still a human.
Failing or falling you are still a human.
Powerless or poverty filled you are still a human.
We are all the images of God.

Black or white you are still a human,
Deaf or blind you are still a human,
With shortage of parts or with all body parts you are
still a human.
Fat or slender you are still a human
Rich or poor you are still a human.
It's a wonderful gift to be a human.

It does not matter your condition,
It does not matter your tradition,
It does not matter your skin complexion
It does not matter your origin
All creations have the purposes to be living.
Judging yourself is a limitation
Limitation is underestimation
Underestimating means to weaken
To weaken means to lose, and to be weak.

Be who you are, never change yourself.
Never and never compere yourself with others
Nothing can change you from being a human.

Questioning

A question is a question.
A question needs an answer,
A question remains being a question if its answer is
not in action.
A question is what every person has.
Why do you need an answer?

Some questions can't change even when we get
answers.
Can you change why you are born in a poor family?
Some questions we can't run from them,
Can you make yourself to be older than your twin?
Let it go.

For many times we want to change the
unchangeable,
For many times we need answer that we have,
For many times we question the things that are in
the hands of life rotation.
What will your answer change?

A question can cause stress
A question can cause illnesses
A question can cause separation,
A question can cause hatred
A question can cause any bad thing,
Why don't you try to accept?

Job said in the bible, ''I came to this earth naked I
will retreat naked''
Life is life, everyone has a question.
The more the questions is the more the stress.
Let you heart be not be troubled.

Death

You are death,
You cause tears and pain
You cause cries and groans
You cause separation and wars
In you there's no life.

Nobody accept you
Nobody loves you
Everybody fight you
Everybody run away from you
Everybody hates you

You are death and you are unfair.
Parents are left with no children
Children are left with no parents
Lovers are left alone and separated

You can't be avoided because you are everywhere

Take action

Don't talk before you do
Don't announce before you made it happen

Think before you do
Don't say you can't without trying
Don't give up easily
Keep your hope alive
Keep your faith strong,

Use your potential
Use your mind
What is needed is your natural ability
Believe in yourself

Don't let people talk you out of your determination
Don't kneel to oppositions
Just as science learners they will tell you that
Actions speak louder than words.
Never announce your moves, before you move

A Dog

A dog is a dangerous animal.
A dog can change its appearance any time
A dog is a good pretender
A dog is a thief
A dog does what benefits itself only
A dog can't smile

A dog shows its teeth when it wants to bite
A dog comes to you as if its smiling
Even if its intention is to bite

When a dog gives you a welcome bark
It doesn't mean it comes in peace

Not every dog that Burks at you will bite

Smile

A smile is simple and created through joy.
A smile can kill your enemies
A smile can bring self -amendment
A smile can amend people near you
Smile black child, smile white child.

Everyone wants to smile where there's joy.
We have to smile even when we are sad
For smile is a weapon in our lives
A smile is a medication in our lives

Never stop smiling.
Even when your enemies smile at you,
Keep on smiling.

Having a smile on your face is a blessing.
You can have money but lack smile
You can eat well but lack smile
You can dress fancy and be beautiful, but lack smile.
You can be talented and educated, but lack smile.
You can be rich or poor, but lack smile.
You can be drive fancy cars and being wealthy, but
lack smile.
Smile black child, smile white child.

Keep on smiling in all conditions only to kill your
enemies.

BROKEN PROMISE

Our first day was like being in heaven.
Our first kiss was like receiving a crown of noble
people; our first touch was like removing all our
problems away from us.

Our first night was like being in another planet where
only I and you existed. We were in the seventh
heaven.

Our first walk together was like that of a king and
queen being guarded by the angels of love.
I wish everything can be like before.

We were living a life of harmony
We were living a life of being led by angels of love.
Love is a feeling and a sense.
I always feel and sense you
I wish everything can be like before.

You promised to be there for me
You promised not to leave me
You promised to be with me in all troubles of life
You promised not to break my heart
Yet now am bleeding because of you.
I wish everything can be like before.

I don't know what!
Is it hard to be faithful?
I don't know why you promised lies.
I don't know why you played my heart with your false promises. I wish things can be normal, but now I see that some wishes can't happen.

The water has been poured already.

Eyes Acts

Eyes see things
Eyes direct people
Eyes communicate
Eyes shows emotions

It is not all what you see that is true. Not all eyes
signs are true. Watch your eyes unless you fall into
trouble

Sometimes people pretend to us, because we
believe in everything we see
We end up believing in what we see.
Sometimes we can see opposite things of the truth.
Don't be deceived by what you see.
They are eyes we control them
They are eyes we move them
Never believe everything you see with your eyes.

FIRST TIME FASCINATION

Oh my GMG! I still wonder if you are real.
Are you touchable?
Do you live here?
Is this a dream or am falling in the garden of love?
You walk like a model angel in the presents of God.
Is this really or just an imagination

Your eyes shine like light puts away darkness
You are so awesome just as your creator in heaven
I am intoxicated by the rhythm of your Veracity
This is a miracle!

I never believed that angels exist until I saw you.
I also believe that heaven and paradise is real.
I never thought I can meet an angel on earth.
Your voice is a music playing in my ears.

Your beauty is tremendous
Your body is noble and elegant
Your eyes blink like a diamond
Truly you're an angel

MY CRUSH

You're the one close to my soul
You're the magnet my heart can't resist.
You're the power of love, the passion that fascinate.

You're the meaning of love in a distance.
Getting you in my life will be like finding my world.

Day and night I think about you
Day and night I wish you can read my mind, before I broadcast with you.

Day and night I fill like my heart is no longer with me when we're apart. You stole it from a distance.

Day and night I dream and image of you.
 I am overwhelmed by your love.
Without your presents there's no glory.
I am passionate about you
I need you; I can't live without you
You are the part am looking for
You are the one needed to complete my life.
I shout to you today, I heart you, be mine forever and ever.

MY DREAM GIRL

She is my joy constructor
My smile maker, my dream girl
She's the flow of my cardiac
The rib of my rib
All I can see is her angelic movement and smiles
She's nothing much but my world.
She's the love angel, the peace creator.

My steps count zero if she's not moving with me.
My smile fades away without her company
She's my heart guardian angel, the rose of my life.

What a nice world filled with an elegant woman.
My heart is like an open hole and you are the water
My heart is deeper than the oceans; your presence
fills it till It overflows.

In your presence my cardiac melt, my ego freeze
Your arms are warmer than any warming regiment.

THE BLIND PERSON

You killed, but you never gained from all the souls.
You destroyed, but you never gained from all.
You became a whore, but you are only left with
regrets. You did all the bad things but none of those
acts made you gain

Being blind while you have eyes is uncommon, but
is happening. Many have eyes, but we are not able
to see. We need to see, not so long the sun will be
dark.

Only God can make people to see, eyes are not
eyes till God open them twice.
Fear and humanity is part of his life strength.
Do you see?
What makes you think you can see?
What do you see in the world?

A Recall to the Past

A day to recall and to relish the past moments
Some days are super positively astonishing
It was a sunny day on the sandy place
We were in a funny park of Dubai.

Smiles and giggles were air moving on the
atmosphere.
Food and drinks were like the lives of a tree.
Everyone had funny and all the plays to relish.
Everything was massive, the mascot shocked many
people. Friends were just so many as if in a stadium

The time was fantastic
Our soul mates were flying in our hearts
No creature wanted to live the park
We were in a funny park of Dubai

Dances and variety of styles were running over and
over the flow. The body of people were in another
planet of enjoyments. We were in a park of smiles
and giggles as I say to what I saw.

www.ingramcontent.com/pod-product-compliance
Lightning Source LLC
Chambersburg PA
CBHW050912120626
46552CB00004B/1527